T0130510

Recognizing the Sign
for
Relationship Keeping

Recognizing the Sign
for
Relationship Keeping

Diane Smith

BALBOA.
PRESS
A DIVISION OF HAY HOUSE

Balboa Press books may be ordered through booksellers or by contacting:

Balboa Press
A Division of Hay House
1663 Liberty Drive
Bloomington, IN 47403
www.balboapress.com
1-(877) 407-4847

ISBN: 978-1-4525-3923-2 (sc)
ISBN: 978-1-4525-3922-5 (ebk)

Printed in the United States of America

Balboa Press rev. date: 09/23/2011

Recognizing The Sign for Relationship Keeping

Relationship, relationship, what does it mean to you? Are we talking about a relationship with a friend, with a boyfriend, with a spouse? Or let's go as far as talking about a relationship with family. What makes people come together, what makes them tear apart? Have you ever wondered why people don't stay together like they used to years ago?

The rate of divorce is so high now, that we are left discouraged at the idea of marriage. Many enter marriage vows wondering if this will last. What has happened in the last 30 years to make us feel that love is no longer forever?

As a little girl, I used to think that LOVE was a magical place, that it was a fairy tale. I looked around myself and found that LOVE was a place where two people got together, got married and had babies, because that's the way it was.

I was born in a family of 12 children. I was the 10th baby of this very poor, French Catholic family. I wore hand-me downs all my life, teased by my older siblings, and school kids. It was very hard to feel confident about myself when I felt and looked poor. We were a family from Quebec, who needed to move to Ontario to find opportunity to work in the fields in order to sustain us. Many nights I would hear my mother crying because they didn't know where the next dollar would come to pay the bills. We would work in the fields from June until October from early hours till dusk. Some of those years we would be kept out of school until October 10th, missing the first month of school. We would show up at school with one new outfit, one new pair of shoes and one month behind all the other students. Moving to Ontario was also difficult with the fact that we didn't speak English. The insecurities that I felt as a child continued.

By the time I was 13, I started to pray to better our lives. My father got a job as a carpenter and my mother got a job in a factory. We moved to a bigger town, and were placed in school after Labour Day. That was exciting, I finally spoke English well, and we started school at the same time as every one else. My first goal was to get my own job and earn my own money. I prayed every night before I slept to get a babysitting job. Within a few weeks I had so many that I had to share them with my younger sister. That's when I started to believe in the magic of prayer.

As I got older, I noticed that when my older siblings turned 18, they got married and moved out of the home. By the time I was 16, I so wanted to fall in love. I prayed regularly to send me a nice guy to marry. My second real boyfriend, from the East end of town, ended up being my husband. Again, as you can predict, I too married at 18. I was the 9th wedding in our family. While in High School, I worked hard to get high marks and my teachers and guidance counsellor had high hopes for me. Retaining a school average of almost 90%, it was expected of me to become something. My family only expected me to turn 18 and move out and get married. There was no money for university expenses in our livelihood. Marriage is all I knew. One day near the end of my grade 13 year, my favourite math teacher asked me which University I planned on attending. I broke down in huge sobs and she put her hand on my shoulder and asked me what was wrong? I told her that I was not sure what I should do, everyone at the school expected me to go on to University but all I wanted to do was get married to Ed. I felt bad due to all the expectations there, but as far as my family was concerned, getting married would be what I would do. I'll never forget her answer, "follow your heart and do what will make YOU happy". At that moment the weight was lifted off my shoulder, I stopped crying and felt a total peace come over me and I knew that marrying Ed would make me happy. And so it was . . .

Most people thought that it was absolutely crazy that I would choose marrying Ed over going away to University. But I felt quite confident about it. I didn't know it then, but my teacher had been sent to me that day to give me this message. She was a messenger of God who answered my prayer. I had been so torn and confused on what to do with my future. Her answer to me has been held close to my heart ever since. This was another reason why I believed in prayer.

Ed and I got married in July, right after grade 13 graduation and have now been married over 33 years. Most people around me would say that we are the perfect couple. I can't say that we are perfect in looks, as we look quite ordinary, but we are perfect in communication and love. We laugh together, we watch the same TV shows together and we love people around us. If you asked us what the secret to our marriage was, we both would answer "communication". Now, we take it one step further, and that is "communication with God".

It was only a few weeks ago that our answer for the secret to a good marriage was still "Communication". But then my friend and I attended a Hayhouse conference in Toronto. Wayne Dyer was a keynote speaker. Doreen Virtue, Cheryl Richardson and Deborah King were also speakers. There were many other speakers, but through this whole seminar, I kept asking myself "what is my purpose?", and in the middle of one of the speaker's workshops, I thought to myself, "you'll be a motivational speaker". I then asked myself, "on what?" and thought, "motivating couples in keeping their relationship strong". This sounded totally crazy to me, as I don't have a degree on the matter, and have had no training with couples. I had to laugh at this idea.

Later in another session at this conference, I thought to myself, "you'll write a book on it", "on what"? I asked myself, what would be the title? "Recognizing the Signs". (I jotted it down in my notepad). I had learned that weekend, that when you pray, the answer comes to you with the speed of sound. So I figured that, those were the answers. It felt weird to me, but once I started to digest the idea, I liked it. Why not? Ed and I have been married 33 years, we are happy together, and we do have a lot to share with other couples.

I got home and told Ed all about the Conference and what idea I came home with. You can imagine that he raised an eyebrow. When I asked him to tell me what his definition of a good marriage was, he said, "communication". I laughed, it was always my definition as well, but after spending the weekend in Toronto at this conference, it came to me, the answer is "prayer". When I shared this with Ed, he didn't disagree with me. It's true, Ed and I have been praying out loud to one another every night when we go to bed. It sounds strange, but one of our agreements when we got married, is not to be shy about praying out loud to one another before going to sleep. As well, we had agreed to not ever go to bed mad. Who could? Even if we ever went to bed mad at each other, after doing a prayer out loud to one another, how could you ever remain mad? This is why I want to share this with couples all over the world.

Later in the book, I will place a few simple prayers that we do together; mainly they are about thankfulness, and blessing people around us, asking for particular help in current situations. They are simple and they usually take one minute each and are powerful. I believe by doing the prayer out loud, that you are technically placing your needs out in the universe. Then the universe answers . . .

Now, lets talk about what LOVE is:

In the bible it says;

> *Love is patient, love is kind. It does not envy, it does not boast, it is not proud. It is not rude, it is not self-seeking, it is not easily angered, it keeps no record of wrongs. Love does not delight in evil but rejoices with the truth. It always protects, always trusts, always hopes, always perseveres. Love never fails. And now these three remain: faith, hope and love. But the greatest of these is love.— excerpts from <u>1 Corinthians 13:4-13</u>*

I remember hearing this at a Church I attended with a friend at Christmas time, and thought it was so beautiful. How true . . . If we always believed in this verse, relationship would be more solid. Years later, I was asked to read this verse at my friend's wedding, and the priest came up to me after, to tell me that I read that verse so beautifully. I didn't realize it at the time, but I guess, that I really believed it.

Sometimes, we get carried away with LOVE. Is it supposed to be magical? Are you supposed to hear fireworks when you kiss?

Is it supposed to be like a fairy tale, where you live happily ever after? With all the movies, the songs, the stories we hear in this day of age, we think that if LOVE is not like those, then we are not really in love. We don't seem to work hard enough to keep it together.

So many of this generation give up on love.

What is LOVE?

What is LOVE to you?

Describe 3 things that LOVE means to you.

1)

2)

3)

Ask your Loved one to do the same.

1)

2)

3)

Love is a complicated thing. We all have a different perception of what love is. For years, I asked myself, am I really "In love"? To this day, I still don't know that I really know the answer to that. I love Ed, but how? He's my best friend, I love to spend lots of time with him, I love to share my day with him, I love to walk on the beach with him, I love to sing to him, I love to watch the birds with him, I love to just be with him. Is that love? Is that enough? Yes, it is. I don't hear bells, I don't see fireworks, but I know that I would not be happy without him. I look forward to doing our prayer together at the end our day.

Next, let's talk about HAPPINESS:

What is happiness? Is it shopping, traveling, eating, holding your baby, going to the movies together, or how big your bank account is?

There are many variables in life that make us happy. The key is, what keeps you happy?

Make a list of 3 things that make you happy.

1)

2)

3)

Ask your loved one the 3 things that make him happy too.

1)

2)

3)

It's OK for you and your partner to not see eye to eye on what love means, or what makes you happy. What makes it OK is the fact that you communicate about it.

Now that I understand that praying out loud with each other is key to helping a marriage, I believe that communication is the second to that. So you want to make sure that you do the above exercise.

Every day I look forward to coming home from work, just to share our day. It's important that you both show interests in each other's day. To be honest with you, I think Ed listens to me 70% of the time, while I listen 30% of the time. That doesn't seem fair, but it works for us. Over the years, we have been on many roller coaster rides. Yes, real roller coasters, our first date, was a "blind date". We went to the fair, and laughed so hard on the "Zipper". It still remains one of our favourite rides. But what I really mean by roller coaster rides, is that our marriage has been a roller coaster.

What could be obstacles in a marriage? Most marriages break up for one of these reasons:

Lack of money, Lack of fidelity, lack of communication, and I'll add "lack of prayer".

Unfortunately, many people joke that the leading cause of divorce is "marriage". Well it's no joke! Marriage should be taken more seriously, and should be worked on with a little more effort.

Let's talk about money. Yes money can bring happiness, but lack of money is very difficult on a marriage.

Ed and I certainly have had our ups and downs where that was concerned. When we were first married, I got a full time job at a plumbing store. It felt like I was working for 2 "Grumpy Old Men". After 8 months of walking on egg shells at my job, I finally walked out and quit. Quitting was very hard on me, and my confidence. I went home and was worried about what I had done. I didn't know what I would tell Ed, when he came home from work.

I remember being in bed, crying and praying for help. After about 15 minutes, I felt a total peace come upon me. I got up, and decided to open up a magazine. All of a sudden, I saw an article that said, "when a door closes, a window opens". I took that as a sign that I was going to be OK. I opened up the newspaper and searched out the job availabilities. Within a few weeks, I had found another job. Better money, better hours, better place.

A few years later, Ed and I started having a family, first a son, who was babysat by Grandma, so that we both could work. Then I got pregnant for our second child, a daughter. That's when I decided that I wanted to be a stay-at-home mom. Luckily, I was introduced to a Home Party business, and decided to resign from my full-time job and do home parties a couple of nights a week so that I could spend my days taking care of my two beautiful children. Again, this was very stressful on our bank account, but together we made this work.

I have been in sales most of our married life. Let me tell you that "sales" is not an easy career. We had months where my commissions were exciting, and then months where the commissions would not cover our basic bills. I have taken many risks over the years, and Ed who had a "steady eddie" job was my backbone. I would always look for that easiest, fastest growing company to work for in sales. My head swelled as I was getting more and more confident with sales. I've made mistakes and it taught us some big lessons.

In 1989, I was on my fifth year with a "Lingerie" company. I had won tons of awards, and won many trips and was making $100,000 a year in commissions. We were having fun and we were spending big. All of a sudden, I was distracted with a new company starting up in Canada. When I joined them, the lingerie company found out and decided to cut me off of my commissions. It was devastating! I was under the impression that I could have done both, but not according to them. We found ourselves financially strapped and we ended up taking them to court. It was a 5-year process and very nerve racking and very expensive. Looking back on it now I wished that we wouldn't have started a lawsuit against them because it slowed down my progress in my new career for those 5 years. It was a huge distraction and we were forced to sell our home, (and luckily it sold). We were forced to downgrade into a smaller house, which was very humiliating. We were forced to borrow money at 29% interest in order to continue to pay the lawyer his ongoing fees.

When all was said and done, the judge granted only a $33,300 settlement. I was so upset, that I ended on the floor in the bedroom sobbing. I couldn't believe that after all that, we didn't win, but got our expenses back. I sobbed so hard, that I was making myself sick. I prayed for help, again, I felt a sense of calmness come over me and I got up and decided that it was OK. We paid our loan, $33,000 lawyer fees and we were left with a measly $300. We bought a dog! At least, the $300 would grow with us, he was a beautiful Sheltie called Casey. His registered name surprisingly was "Dream Come True". I took that as a sign, and starting that day, we decided to move forward and start a new life, with the weight of that lawsuit off our shoulders.

Over those 5 years, there had been many tears, many fights and many doubts. But I truly believe that our prayers out loud each night, guided us through. Our communication with each other, helped soothe our hurt. We sat down the night we got our dog, and after tucking in our children, we took all the transcripts from the court case (which were 2 huge boxes), and proceeded to open up a bottle of wine, and lit the fireplace. We sat back talking and laughing, while the transcripts burned. It was our way to cleanse the past and a great exercise to help us move forward. This had been a great test in our lives, but our marriage was stronger from the experience.

What does MONEY mean to you?

1)

2)

3)

What does it mean to your partner?

1)

2)

3)

Would you believe that I didn't learn my lesson? You would think that after downgrading to a smaller house, swallowing my pride, no longer making $100,000/year, and going through a huge lawsuit, that I would be more careful not to find myself in a financial situation again. Not so, here we go again....Life is not easy!

I started with a great sales company selling herbs, and again I built this business up to $100,000/year. So again, we bought a huge home and we were so happy there. I got distracted again with a new business coming into Canada.

We found ourselves in financial trouble again. This time, our house wasn't selling. We didn't know what to do. Our real estate agent suggested that we might have to go see a Bankruptcy Trustee to get out of our mess. I couldn't fathom that.

My pride was too strong and there was no way that we were going through this again . . . We finally made the decision that we had to jump; it was so hard on us. One day, when the kids were in school, and Ed was at work, I found myself breaking down. I laid on the couch, sobbing and praying for help. This time, I was in a fetal position, not knowing what we would do. All of a sudden, the phone rang. One of my daughter's teachers called. I had not talked to this teacher in years. My daughter was graduating grade 8, and the class was going to a retreat for the day to prepare for her Confirmation day. The teacher calling me was in charge of this church retreat. She called to ask me if I wouldn't mind helping her that day with the retreat. I pulled myself together, and said sure. It turns out it was the Friday before we moved out and decided to abandon our beautiful home. Even though I was totally stressed and in the middle of packing, I said yes.

That day, on the retreat, we were all split into smaller groups. I was in charge of six students. We were all given a card with a quote from the bible. We were supposed to go outside and take a picture of what we thought the quote meant. Our card said: *"Come to me, all you who are weary and burdened, and I will give you rest". Matthew 11:28-30*

I proceeded to take the students outside to sit on a park bench, lay their backpacks on the ground, and lean their heads on each other. It was a fun exercise. After lunch, this teacher, who had called me, started her talk. She asked the students, "where is God?" The students replied, "in our priest, in our teachers, in our parents". She agreed, "yes, God speaks through all of them and sometimes He speaks through a stranger who was sent to give you a message." All of a sudden I realized that the quote that we worked on, was my message. I left the room, went to the washroom and cried. My message was to trust God with my heavy burden, and let him take care of it. I then understood that it was OK to walk away from our financial burden and move forward. This realization was so strong, that it took me a few minutes to pull myself together, I washed my face, felt a calmness come over me, and proceeded to walk out and continue my day helping the students as if nothing had happened.

We moved that Sunday afternoon, we had a heavy heart, but we knew that the message had helped us move forward to build up our lives. It was hard, probably the hardest obstacle that we ever faced as a married couple. But again, making us stronger together. We kept the communication going, and our nightly prayers with each other.

On the same day that we signed our Bankruptcy papers, I got a new job. I heard a job ad on the radio and it stopped me in my tracks. I wrote the phone number down, attended an interview and was offered the job. My prayers were answered and we were once again on the road to recovery.

Yes, money can be the biggest obstacle in a marriage, communication about it is key, but communication about it to God is the secret.

Lack of FIDELITY:

It seems to be the second biggest reason for a marriage to fail. I can't say that I relate to this one. As I said at the beginning, Ed and I are pretty ordinary looking people. So attracting others has never been a problem for us. I have a theory about that. It doesn't matter what you look like, lack of fidelity has no boundaries. So what causes it? We could use many excuses, and that's exactly what they are, excuses. How do you avoid it? It's simple . . .

If you agree to pray out loud each night together, how could you be unfaithful?

During that one-minute prayer, your true self comes out, the honesty comes out, and the prayer for help comes out. If you believe that you are struggling as a couple, you pray about it, put it out in the universe, and be patient, be faithful to yourselves, and watch what happens. I truly believe that through the years, temptation has come our way, but because of our commitment to pray at night, we didn't recognize the temptations, and we certainly didn't look for them. We focused on keeping our marriage strong, rather than looking for excuses for the marriage not to work.

What are some of the excuses that people use to be unfaithful?

1) Sex or lack of sex
2) Working too many hours
3) Drinking too much
4) Ignoring each other through the children
5) Anger issues, abuse

6) In-Laws interference
7) Jealousy
8) Health issues
9) Addictions
10) Controlling issues

The above are some of the reasons and the dark sides that hurt a marriage, there's no doubt. Unfortunately, these are excuses used to be unfaithful. Most of these lead to lack of fidelity, which is the 2nd biggest reason why marriages fail. What if I was here to tell you, that all of the above could be solved with one simple act? Yes, as I said before, you pray together, each night, out loud. Is it too late to start? Will it really work? Are you willing to commit to that? What if you did?

What is your goal? You would not have purchased this book, if you didn't want to help your marriage or your relationship. What if it was that simple? It sounds too good to be true? Could you try it for 21 days? We've heard it many times, that it takes 21 days to form a habit. What if you committed to going to bed at the same time for 21 days? You lay on your back together and one starts their prayer, and then the other one does theirs. Does that sound difficult? Does a breakup or visit at the divorce lawyer sound easier?

Ed and I have been doing these since our first night together. Sometimes we giggle on who will go first, but over the years, we've decided, I go first. It's fun, and easy. Trust me, sometimes, Ed falls asleep before my prayer is done, and I have to elbow him to wake him up and do his. Most times, I daydream through his. Sometimes, he mumbles his. Sometimes, I do mine alone, because he watches a Playoff

Hockey game. That's OK, as long as he promises that he does his before he falls asleep. Just get it out there in the Universe.

Once the prayer is done, we sleep like babies through the night. It is a great way to end the day on a positive note. We rarely fight before going to bed and it's hard to stay mad after a prayer. But trust me, we've had our share of angry nights, where we refuse to do our prayer together, so we do it silently apart. But to tell you the truth, after doing my prayer, I feel bad about our fight, and I turn around and snuggle him, and say I'm sorry. It's then automatically forgotten and it's OK, we move on. It somehow erases the anger and replaces it with forgiveness. It magically is better. I never understood it, but it works.

You may think that I'm very religious. I can't say that I am overly religious, but I do believe in a higher power. Yes, we've agreed to continue to go to church every Sunday, as our parents did. But, we don't participate in any church activities. We are the couple that shows up every Sunday, but pretty well invisible. What I love best about going to church is that I enjoy my one-on-one with God, as I kneel. I also find praying at home, just as powerful.

Nowadays, church is becoming a place of prayer for the older generation. It seems that the congregations are older. There are not many younger families attending. Even my children do not go to church anymore, since they left for University. My daughter once said, that she was a "Chreaster". I asked what that was, and she responded that it's people that go to church only at Christmas and Easter. I laughed, but it really isn't funny. What happened to kneeling at the bed before going to sleep? What happened to doing grace before a meal? We have forgotten how to pray. The younger generation has become disillusioned with church. They don't feel like it serves a purpose. What do we do as parents?

Let them pray their own way may be the only solution. We can't make them go, we can't make them feel guilty, but if we encourage them to spend 1 minute at the end of their day to thank God and to pray to God, then that's all we can ask for now.

So, what is a PRAYER?

It can be as simple as a "Thank You" message at the end of the day.

It can be as simple as a request for guidance, for help, for protection. As I mentioned earlier, I learned that a prayer is answered as fast as "the speed of sound". The question is, are we listening???? What are you listening for? How about the thought that came in your mind, when you asked the question? That is probably the answer, go with it, trust the thought, it's your intuition, your gut feeling, your answer. Are you listening????

Examples of prayers:

> *Thank you God for this wonderful day, thank you for my wonderful husband that I love so very much. Thank you for our beautiful children, please keep them safe, healthy and wise in all the decisions that they make. Please watch over my parents and Ed's dad, and keep them happy and healthy. Please make that I will have a successful day tomorrow with my work, and that we will have a good week ahead of us. Thank you for everything, and please watch over all our friends and family. We love you very much for watching over us, Amen.*

What is key in this prayer? It's just off the top of our heads, whatever comes to mind for that moment. To be in a state of thankfulness is the most important. Thanking for a "wonderful" husband is secondly important, because by saying it out loud, you are confirming to your partner that he is "wonderful" and that "you love him very much". How can a partner doubt your love when you profess it to God every night? I truly believe that praying to keep my children safe is the 3rd most important thing in my life. And then I pray for whatever is pertaining to our lives in the moment.

No matter what happens in your daily lives, pray about it before you go to bed. It is then placed in the Universe. The Universe does not know the difference between a positive or negative statement. So keep your prayers positive and expect positive results.

For example: If you pray and you say, *please help me with my drinking problem,*

The universe hears "drinking problem" and can't understand why you need help. How about switching the words to "please help me to not drink alcohol tomorrow, so that I can be stronger at making the right decisions". It's important to talk about yourself in a positive way, and make positive statements.

More examples:

> *Thank you God for all that you bring to our lives. Thank you for my wonderful life, my wonderful husband and our beautiful kids. Please keep them safe and smart. Help Jeremy in all of his decisions, so that he makes the right decisions in his life. Please take care of our aging parents. Keep them healthy and happy. Watch over all our friends that we care about. Please make that my day will be successful tomorrow in my job. Protect our home and our livelihood. We thank you for everything you do for us. We love you very much for watching over us. Amen*

The prayer takes on a similar look every night. Acknowledging and thanking God for everything that he does for us is great. Asking for guidance and protection is important. And asking on behalf of someone else like your children or friends or family is also good.

Practice a couple of your own prayers:

1)

2)

Nobody wants their marriage to FAIL:

Remember how you felt when you first met and remember how you felt on your wedding day? What happened? Life happened! Sometimes life can feel like it's spitting you out. It is how you deal with it and what you do about it that transforms into a happy marriage. No one said it would be easy, as a matter of fact there is not one book out there that tells you how to live your life perfectly. It would be impossible to have your life mapped out. The job, the children, the pets, the distractions, the disappointments are all part of life. That's life! But you have free will. Yes, you have a choice, you can choose to work on it, or choose not to. I was told years ago that the first two things you should do in the morning, is make up your bed, and make up your mind to have a good day. This helps you start the day off on the right foot. Then as the day progresses, you choose to make right decisions, eat the right foods, be nice to people, and of course be nice to your partner.

Whenever we argue, I try to put myself in his shoes and then I feel bad for him, so I soften up. It's hard to stay mad. Again, you can choose to stay mad, but what will that accomplish? It makes it so hard to reconnect again. Make it a rule not to be mad more than one-hour max. If you ask God to help you, you will feel calmer and make up. Just a small nudge, a look, a smile, a hug, can make a world of difference.

Forgiveness is so hard sometimes. How do you begin to forgive when you feel so hurt? Harsh words have been said that cannot be taken back, actions are done that cannot be undone. Again you can choose to forgive or you can choose to fester on it forever.

Who are you hurting when you fester and can't forgive?

You are only hurting yourself! It's hard to remain positive when you feel down, hurt and betrayed. You need to get it out of your system.

This is a small exercise that you can do to remove the hurt. Write your partner a letter. This can also be done for anyone that you can't forgive, be it a parent, a child, a friend, a family member, a boss, or your partner. It works each time. You prepare to write a letter, be in a calm state, go to a quiet room, and do a short prayer for help in using the right words to help you forgive. Pour your feelings out in this letter, take 4 pages or take10. It doesn't matter, but you must tell this person in the letter that you forgive him. When you are done, either burn it or throw it out while doing a short prayer. Have you forgiven this person? Yes, and now you can move forward. As long as the intention is there, and you've put it in writing, it is now in the Universe. Allow the Universe to heal you now.

The key is this; it doesn't matter if the person ever knows that you have forgiven them. You never have to speak to them again; you don't even have to be their friend as long as you have forgiven them. You will feel a sense of relief; you now can heal your hurt. It's about your well being that you needed to forgive, because anger can make you sick. Now if this letter is written to your partner, you should be able to feel the sense of relief immediately and move forward with your relationship. Don't believe me? Give it a try! Then continue to do your nightly prayers and continue to use positive words in your prayers.

What about SEX?:

Definitely, sex is an integral part of a marriage. This can be the most sensitive part of a happy marriage. Sometimes, we take sex too seriously. The key here is communication!!!!!! What are you comfortable with, what are you not comfortable with? Does he know? Do you know what he wants? Do you feel like you have to? Do you feel like you want to?

When you communicate how you feel, what your needs are, how you want to do it, when you want to do it, can help greatly in the relationship. Some people can go years without communicating to their partner what they don't like about their sexual feelings. Reading books on it, and experiencing new positions, new places, and enjoying each other's company is so important.

When was the last time you went parking or did it on the beach, or in the rain, or on the back deck? When was the last time you bought new lingerie, used marital toys, had a bath together, or lit candles in the bedroom? These are all ways to make it intimate and fun.

We used to spend Sunday afternoons, playing cards on the bed. Dealer's choice of what game was played, loser took off one piece of clothing and then back to the game again, until you had built such anticipation that love-making was amazing. We still spend some Sunday afternoons playing cards on the bed. It's great fun!!!!

We used to laugh when we went to bed, because we couldn't decide if we should do our prayer before or after lovemaking. Just go with your gut on that one, but it is better to do your prayer after, as the prayer takes on more of a sentimental take.

Now, I'm going to tell you that I am not a sex therapist. I think we get too hung up on whether an orgasm is attained during sex. My question to you is that, does it really matter? Does that make or break a marriage? It shouldn't!

According to research 50-75% of women don't reach orgasm each time they have sex. Is that a good enough reason for a marriage to go bad? It doesn't have to be. Choose to enjoy your partner in the best way possible, and don't put such emphasis on the lack of orgasm. Enjoy each other!!!!

Here's a small exercise for both of you:

What are some of your expectations in love making?

1)

2)

3)

What are some of his expectations in love making?

1)

2)

3)

CHILDREN and the fun it adds to a marriage:

Wow, what a subject . . . children and the new fun it adds to the marriage. Boy, I could write a whole book about this subject. One thing for sure, it's easy to love your kids unconditionally. Again, you choose to love them unconditionally. I thank God that we didn't have a hard marriage with raising our kids. We had our share of obstacles. First, coming home from the hospital with our beautifully wrapped up baby in his new clothes. The minute we put him down in his brand new basinet he proceeded to have a bowel movement that ran right through his diaper, his new clothes and his basinet. Ouch! Welcome home! We both stood there and looked at each other and thought; we have to clean this??? What a mess.

We were the perfect parents, taking our son to all his sports; soccer, baseball, hockey, basketball and tae kwon do. Whew, busy!!!

We took our daughter to her ballet lessons and her piano lessons.

We had the perfect family.

But don't let me kid you; we went through our share of disappointments and frustrations. Our son was a great kid, so joyful and so full of energy. When he turned 17 we lost him. We lost him to a girl and he lost his virginity. We lost him to alcohol and drugs. Boys will be boys, so it wouldn't be right if he didn't experience these things. We prayed for him and always prayed that he would be safe and so he was. The police came over a couple of times, once because he had punched a guy out cold in front of a bar, and once because he was caught defacing proof of age cards.

Luckily both times no charges were laid. Off he went to University and managed to stay out of trouble, but drinking, drugs and girls were a huge part of his University days. We paid tuition for his 4 years University, but while at University we encouraged him to work, so he could have "entertainment" money. Well, he enjoyed the job so well that he continued in that field, and his University days were not used for a good career. So as much as we love our son to death, we can't say that we are very proud of what he does today. But every night we pray that he is happy, healthy and wise in the decisions that he makes. According to him, he is very happy, and he is very healthy, as he eats better foods than we do. As for being wise, we question that fact, but according to him, he thinks he's making wise decisions. So what is his career that he is so wise about? While at university, he chose to work at a strip bar as a waiter. A few years later he became a dancer.

He feels admired on those 2-3 nights a week that he works and that makes him very happy. On is 4-5 days off, he gets to sleep, eat and work out so that his body looks perfect. It's definitely not the kind of life we dreamed of for our son, but we leave it in God's hands, and I'm sure that somehow, someway, we trust that there is a good reason why he is on this journey. He is now 29 and I keep saying that the "umbilical cord" has been cut off, and he is his own man now and he seems to be happy, so we have to be happy for him.

As for our beautiful daughter, she has been an angel all her life. We did go through a stage when she was 14-15 where she had us worried. Which 15 year old out there doesn't worry her parents? Our sweet little angel found herself caught up in an Internet situation with an older guy. We assumed she was chatting with people that she knew every time she logged in. For 3 years she communicated with an older fella from California who gave her 1 800 calling card #'s so she could call him from the school pay phone. They chatted on the phone for years, and on the Internet. She was sweet and innocent and very vulnerable, as so many young girls are today. Luckily, as far as we know, they never met. We caught her one morning when she was wearing a diamond necklace that we hadn't given to her. This brought the whole thing out in the open. After a whole day of interrogating her and stripping her bedroom for any signs of information that would lead us to him, we found his address. We sent the necklace back, threatening to turn him into the police. She never heard from him again, but in her fantasy world, she was in love with him and we feared that she had planned on running away to meet him soon. Thankfully she hadn't actually planned on running away. We thank God that he answered our prayers, and kept her safe, by showing us that necklace in the nick of time. She is now a 26-year old young woman with a good job and a nice boyfriend. We pray for the best for her, as she definitely lights up our world.

Children can be a joy, but they can also cause the most worrisome days of your lives. How you deal with each situation and how you communicate together can definitely change any outcome. Remember that these new generations need our prayers. They don't seem to believe in the power of prayer. They watch too much TV, read too many articles that create them to be very indifferent and cynical to a higher power. Unfortunately, some of that generation now believes that vampire stories have bigger power over them than God. We need to stay positive that somehow, with our prayers, these children of ours will keep on the right path in their lives.

It's not always easy to be a parent, but it's very rewarding. That kind of love is unconditional.

What is happening to the children in broken homes? There are too many of them. I can't even imagine what it would have been like to have my children be part of a broken home.

I respect the single moms and dads out there that deal with separation when the child goes away every other weekend to see the other parent. My heart would absolutely break for them. How do we stop this? How do we keep a family together? How do we keep those children protected so that they never have to feel confused at having two homes? Is there a way to help your relationship, your home, and your children from going through life and having to "just get used to it"?

Well, I believe that just by reading this far into this book means that you have a desire to not become one of the statistics out there. What can you do to protect your family and keep it growing together?

What about HEALTH ISSUES?

I won't pretend that I know the difficulties in dealing with a sick loved one. We have had our share of sicknesses such as colds, asthma, and bladder attack. But we haven't had to deal with alcoholism, cancer, and other serious diseases. It takes a strong person to deal with that. My friend was married to a man for 13 years who had had over seven operations on his brain. I can't even imagine dealing with the stress in a marriage with one brain operation, let alone seven on one gentle human being. He put up a courageous fight! It became too much of a strain in the marriage to live with and take care of two growing boys and financially supporting the family. She finally couldn't do it anymore and basically ran away from the situation. It was a shock to everyone, but she felt for her own well being that she needed to move on with her own life. What happened there? The communication stopped?

The strain of the marriage became unbearable? Can she be blamed for leaving? No one walked in her shoes, and her shoes were weighing her down. What might have been missing? Prayer? Could it be that simple? We'll never know. I know that I am thankful that I was never put in a situation like that. I can only imagine the strength that they both needed to keep a marriage strong with all those obstacles. There are many situations across the world like that. We all know the wedding vows say: "Through sickness and health". Only you can decide what to do in a situation where sickness stops the love that you once felt for each other the day you took those vows. But don't hesitate to ask God for help, and pray for the strength to handle any situation together. Remember, when you ask a question, God (the Universe) sends the answer at the speed of sound, the question is, are you listening?

What about CONTROLLING ISSUES?

When you enter into a marriage, you want to have a 50/50 relationship. A give and take is important. Sharing household chores, bank accounts and children responsibilities is part of the teamwork. Of course it all needs to be discussed and agreed upon. Sometimes a controlling spouse comes into the picture, and that also needs to be talked about. It's OK to have your own opinions. It's OK to share and delegate. It's healthy to have your own space. Again if the relationship is important to you, discussion is key.

What causes control issues? Distrust, jealousy and fear play a huge part of control issues and these are very dark emotions. Usually, nothing good comes from these dark emotions. They are very destructive to any relationship. Whether these emotions are felt in a family, a workplace, or in a relationship. Most of these feelings are created because of fear. What is the biggest fear of all? It's the fear of losing your partner. Why is there a fear to begin with? If the love is there from both sides, then there should automatically be trust. Don't allow the dark sides of each other to come out, the jealousy and the distrust that creates fear. Assume a perfect life together and be each other's best friend. Pray about it together, this is no joking matter. If you need assistance in this matter don't be afraid to ask God for guidance.

Taking TIME FOR YOURSELF

It's important to have your own hobbies. Does he want to spend some time with his friends, do you? Sports are a big part of a man's world. It does compete for your time there is no doubt. There are so many sports being televised now, that if a man that loves sports could watch it all, he wouldn't be able to get up and see life. Between hockey, football, basketball, baseball, soccer, UFC, and poker, you may never see your husband ever again.

Again, what can I say? He needs his space, as long as it is in moderation. Discuss it as a team and come to an agreement on what fits your lifestyle. You also need your own space, whether it is going out with a friend, shopping or taking scrap-booking classes, etc. We need that space from one another. Respect that and plan it together.

The HONEYMOON should never be over!

Life is what you make it, if you are ready for life together "till death do you part", then be prepared for the honeymoon to never end. Have fun together, play together and laugh together. The honeymoon is not about being in Hawaii for the rest of your life, but you can bring "Hawaii" to your home. Set some special dates to create your own little honeymoon, set a candlelight dinner, run a bath for the two of you, book a hotel for a night or get a hot tub and share it regularly together. Make the best of what comes your way, and make it happen together!

Be each other's BEST FRIEND:

Who is your best friend? We can have many best friends. Your mother can be your best friend, you friend since childhood can be your best friend, your sister can be your best friend. But most important of all, your partner needs to be your best friend and remember to say "I Love you" often.

I am thrilled to say, I have many good friends, but my best friend of all is my husband. I look forward to seeing him when we come home from work. We kiss goodbye in the morning, we kiss hello when I walk in the house, we hold hands at the movies and we hold hands in church. I tell him absolutely everything, and he shares everything with me too. It's very easy to be honest with each other when we are so close. I feel really close to him, and he feels really close to me. I love my best friend!

Go on DATES and have fun:

Plan dates regularly, because after a hard week's work you may be stressed. Going out to have fun always keeps the spice in the marriage. You can go bowling, go dancing, go to the movies, stop in a coffee shop for a piece of dessert or just take a nice ride to the beach.

Having friends to go out with can also be fun.

It's important as a couple to share your lives with friends and be around other people. Join a card league, hobby groups, sports teams, or do volunteer work in your church or non-profit groups.

Having other interests out in your community is good for your relationship.

Spend some good old family time together:

Turn off the TV and make plans to go out! Take a long ride to a conservation area and go bird watching, take the kids camping, take them to a zoo, take them for ice cream. It's nice to spend family time together to talk about all kinds of things and bond closer.

We used to spend the early spring Sunday afternoons taking the kids to the National Park close by and drive through to count deer. It became a yearly tradition for us. It was sad the first year the kids said that they didn't want to go anymore. Yes, you guessed it they were getting too old. I remember the day my daughter said she didn't want to go to the movies with parents, or go into a mall with me. Wow, what an ego buster! I thought I was her favourite person all along, but my baby had grown up into an adolescent and it was no longer cool to walk in the mall or go to movies with your parents. Never take those special moments for granted, as they grow up so fast. Remember to tell them how much you love them as often as you can.

LAUGHTER is the best medicine:

It's been said forever and ever, "Laughter is the best medicine". Laughing together is a cleansing of the soul. Find funny things to talk about, find ways to laugh at your problems. Laughter reduces stress, it relaxes your whole body and it's fun, free and it's easy to do.

I must to tell you, knowing that our son is a dancer in bars makes us very uncomfortable. My husband to this day still has a hard time with it, but we laugh about it. It reduces the stress we feel about it. My husband responds to it by joking, "He's living my dream"! We laugh at that and move on with our own lives.

Make your life as fun and funny as you can. It's hard being happy when you're stressed, and when you are angry. Make jokes in an uncomfortable situation, to allow laughter to take over a foul mood because laughter will heal that mood.

Take long walks on the beach:

Whether it is on a beach, in a park or in your neighbourhood, make plans to go for walks together, take deep breaths and smell the roses. Fresh air is such a gift. It clears the mind and keeps you healthy. Walks are the easiest form of exercise, but most importantly, hold hands, talk, laugh and share your day and share your dreams together. It's so easy to be best friends when you share moments like that on a regular basis. If you have to, get a dog, you'll have no choice but to take it out for a walk, and do it together.

Follow this simple secret!

Expect to grow old together. What is the secret? I have mentioned it many times in this book. The secret is simple: Pray together out loud to one another every night.

I asked my daughter to help me out and asked her to start this very simple task with her boyfriend. Her first response was, "Mom, I haven't prayed for years! Why should I start now? And by the way, you know my boyfriend doesn't believe in God!"

My answer to that was?

First of all, what is God? Do you believe in a Higher Power? Do you believe in a Higher Power in the Universe? Do you believe in your "Gut feeling" What if your "Gut Feeling" was part of the Universe answering your question? What if the Universe answering your question came from a Higher Power? What if the Higher Power is God?

So I said to her, how about you have a one-minute conversation out loud with each other asking the Universe for guidance and answers to your concerns of the day, and thanking the Universe for everything in your lives? You don't have to call it a "prayer". Would that be awkward or difficult?

Could you do it for 21 days, to form a habit? Could you handle this little exercise? She said she would try . . .

My question to you is this; how badly do you want to grow old together? What have you got to lose?

Lastly, take a look at the cover:

Recognizing The Sign For Relationship Keeping:

This book is a sign to you; it has come into your life at this moment for a reason.

Do you recognize the sign on the cover? The woman's sign has a cross below it, the man's sign points upwards and the two symbols are intertwined together. Recognizing the Sign . . . that this symbol is giving you the secret to Relationship Keeping . . . . "Pray Together, Stay Together".